THE BOOK OF RUTH

ISBN: 979-8-9855655-4-6

Published by Radical, Inc.

RUTH HAS ALL THE ELEMENTS OF A LOVE STORY. TRAGEDY. LOSS. DESPAIR. HOPE. TRIUMPH. LOYALTY. ROMANCE. BUT IT'S MORE THAN JUST A LOVE STORY. IT'S A STORY WITHIN A STORY. IT'S A STORY NOT JUST ABOUT RUTH, BUT ABOUT ALL OF US AND A WORLD IN NEED OF REDEMPTION. AND IN THE END, **WE CAN'T WAIT TO SHOW YOU HOW YOUR STORY IS A PART OF THIS STORY.**

TABLE OF

CONTENTS

Introduction.. 03

About David Platt.. 16

About Radical.. 17

Session 1 | Ruth 1.. 18

Session 2 | Ruth 2.. 36

Session 3 | Ruth 3.. 54

Session 4 | Ruth 4.. 68

Answer Key.. 90

AMONG THE UNREACHED FOR THE UNREACHED

RADICAL.NET/TRAINING

APPLY
TODAY

RI TRAINING

ARTICLES, MESSAGES, SECRET CHURCH ARCHIVES, VIDEOS & MORE

RADICAL.NET

NEIGHBORHOODS & NATIONS

A DOCUMENTARY SERIES EXAMINING GOD'S WORK
IN DIFFICULT PLACES AROUND THE WORLD

YOUTUBE.COM/@FOLLOWRADICAL

BOOKSTORE.RADICAL.NET

FIND THOUSANDS OF BOOKS AND BIBLES AT DISCOUNT PRICES

MAKE CHRIST KNOWN AMONG THE UNREACHED

GIVE TODAY

URGENTNEEDS.ORG

APPAREL WITH PURPOSE

TONIGHT YOUR GENEROSITY CAN FUEL GOSPEL GROWTH IN RED ZONES.

RADICAL.NET/SCGIVE

10 ESSENTIAL TRUTHS EVERY CHRISTIAN SHOULD KNOW AND SHARE ·······································

DAVID PLATT

David Platt serves as a pastor in metro Washington, D.C. He is the founder of Radical.

David received his Ph.D. from New Orleans Baptist Theological Seminary and is the author of *Don't Hold Back, Radical, Follow Me, Counter Culture, Something Needs to Change, Before You Vote,* as well as multiple volumes of the *Christ-Centered Exposition Commentary* series.

Along with his wife and children, David lives in the Washington, D.C., metro area.

RADICAL

Jesus calls us to make his glory known among all the nations by making disciples and multiplying churches. Being on mission is not a program, but the calling of our lives as Christians.

However 3.2 billion people are currently unreached with the gospel, and many of them endure unimaginable suffering. And, only 1% of missions dollars and 3% of missionaries go to the unreached. Something has to change.

Radical exists to equip Christians to be on mission. We serve the church by equipping Christians to **follow Jesus** and to **make him known** in their neighborhoods and among all nations. In places where the gospel is already accessible, we work to **awaken** and **mobilize** the church. In areas where access is limited, we work to **advance the gospel** and **see churches planted.**

SESSION 1 | RUTH 1

NAOMI WIDOWED

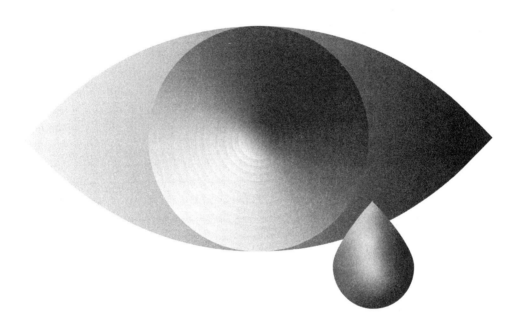

....
....
....
....
....
....
....
....
....
....
....
....
....
....
....
....
....
....
....
....
....
....
....
....
....

Ruth 1:1

[1] In the days when the judges ruled there was a famine in the land, and a man of Bethlehem in Judah went to sojourn in the country of Moab, he and his wife and his two sons.

Genesis

Exodus

Leviticus

Numbers

Deuteronomy

Joshua

Judges

Ruth

1 Samuel

2 Samuel

1 Kings

2 Kings

1 Chronicles

2 Chronicles

Ezra

Nehemiah

Esther

Judges 21:25

25 In those days there was no king in Israel.

Everyone did what was right in his own eyes.

Genesis 19:30-37

30 Now Lot went up out of Zoar and lived in the

hills with his two daughters, for he was afraid

to live in Zoar. So he lived in a cave with his

two daughters. 31 And the firstborn said to the

younger, "Our father is old, and there is not a

man on earth to come in to us after the manner

of all the earth. 32 Come, let us make our father

drink wine, and we will lie with him, that we may

preserve offspring from our father." 33 So they

made their father drink wine that night. And the

firstborn went in and lay with her father. He did

not know when she lay down or when she arose.

34 The next day, the firstborn said to the younger,

"Behold, I lay last night with my father. Let us

make him drink wine tonight also. Then you go in

and lie with him, that we may preserve offspring

from our father." [35] So they made their father drink wine that night also. And the younger arose and lay with him, and he did not know when she lay down or when she arose. [36] Thus both the daughters of Lot became pregnant by their father. [37] The firstborn bore a son and called his name Moab. He is the father of the Moabites to this day.

Numbers 25:1-3

[1] While Israel lived in Shittim, the people began to whore with the daughters of Moab. [2] These invited the people to the sacrifices of their gods, and the people ate and bowed down to their gods. [3] So Israel yoked himself to Baal of Peor. And the anger of the LORD was kindled against Israel.

Deuteronomy 23:3

[3] "No Ammonite or Moabite may enter the assembly of the LORD. Even to the tenth generation, none of them may enter the assembly of the LORD forever,

Ruth 1:2

[2] The name of the man was Elimelech and the name of his wife Naomi, and the names of his two sons were Mahlon and Chilion. They were Ephrathites from Bethlehem in Judah. They went into the country of Moab and remained there.

Ruth 1:3-5

[3] But Elimelech, the husband of Naomi, died, and she was left with her two sons. [4] These took Moabite wives; the name of the one was Orpah and the name of the other Ruth. They lived there about ten years, [5] and both Mahlon and Chilion died, so that the woman was left without her two sons and her husband.

....

....

....

....

....

....

....

....

....

....

....

....

....

....

....

....

....

....

....

....

....

....

....

....

Ruth 1:6

⁶ Then she arose with her daughters-in-law to return from the country of Moab, for she had heard in the fields of Moab that the LORD had visited his people and given them food.

Ruth 1:7

⁷ So she set out from the place where she was with her two daughters-in-law, and they went on the way to return to the land of Judah.

Ruth 1:8-10

⁸ But Naomi said to her two daughters-in-law, "Go, return each of you to her mother's house. May the LORD deal kindly with you, as you have dealt with the dead and with me. ⁹ The LORD grant that you may find rest, each of you in the house of her husband!" Then she kissed them, and they lifted up their voices and wept. ¹⁰ And they said to her, "No, we will return with you to your people."

Ruth 1:11-13

[11] But Naomi said, "Turn back, my daughters; why will you go with me? Have I yet sons in my womb that they may become your husbands? [12] Turn back, my daughters; go your way, for I am too old to have a husband. If I should say I have hope, even if I should have a husband this night and should bear sons, [13] would you therefore wait till they were grown? Would you therefore refrain from marrying? No, my daughters, for it is exceedingly bitter to me for your sake that the hand of the LORD has gone out against me."

....
....
....
....
....
....
....
....
....
....
....
....
....
....
....
....
....
....
....
....
....
....
....
....

Deuteronomy 25:5-6

5 "If brothers dwell together, and one of them dies and has no son, the wife of the dead man shall not be married outside the family to a stranger. Her husband's brother shall go in to her and take her as his wife and perform the duty of a husband's brother to her. 6 And the first son whom she bears shall succeed to the name of his dead brother, that his name may not be blotted out of Israel.

Ruth 1:14

14 Then they lifted up their voices and wept again. And Orpah kissed her mother-in-law, but Ruth clung to her.

Genesis 2:24

24 Therefore a man shall leave his father and his mother and hold fast to his wife, and they shall become one flesh.

Ruth 1:15

¹⁵ And she said, "See, your sister-in-law has gone back to her people and to her gods; return after your sister-in-law."

Ruth 1:16-17

¹⁶ But Ruth said, "Do not urge me to leave you or to return from following you. For where you go I will go, and where you lodge I will lodge. Your people shall be my people, and your God my God. ¹⁷ Where you die I will die, and there will I be buried. May the LORD do so to me and more also if anything but death parts me from you."

Ruth 1:18

¹⁸ And when Naomi saw that she was determined to go with her, she said no more.

....

....

....

....

....

....

....

....

....

....

....

....

....

....

....

....

....

....

....

....

....

....

....

....

Ruth 1:19

¹⁹ So the two of them went on until they came to Bethlehem. And when they came to Bethlehem, the whole town was stirred because of them. And the women said, "Is this Naomi?"

Ruth 1:20-21

²⁰ She said to them, "Do not call me Naomi; call me Mara, for the Almighty has dealt very bitterly with me. ²¹ I went away full, and the LORD has brought me back empty. Why call me Naomi, when the LORD has testified against me and the Almighty has brought calamity upon me?"

Ruth 1:22a

²² So Naomi returned, and Ruth the Moabite her daughter-in-law with her, who returned from the country of Moab.

A story about two places:

Bethlehem: a land of _____ .

Moab: a land of _____ .

A story of two people:

Naomi: a woman with honest _____ .

Ruth: a woman with humble _____ .

Ruth 1:16-17

¹⁶ But Ruth said, "Do not urge me to leave you or to return from following you. For where you go I will go, and where you lodge I will lodge. Your people shall be my people, and your God my God. ¹⁷ Where you die I will die, and there will I be buried. May the LORD do so to me and more also if anything but death parts me from you."

....

....

....

....

....

....

....

....

....

....

....

....

....

....

....

....

....

....

....

....

....

....

....

....

A story with two points of need:

They needed _____ .

They needed _____ .

Ruth 1:20-21

---

[20] She said to them, "Do not call me Naomi; call me Mara, for the Almighty has dealt very bitterly with me. [21] I went away full, and the LORD has brought me back empty. Why call me Naomi, when the LORD has testified against me and the Almighty has brought calamity upon me?"

Two pictures of God:

He is _____ .

He is _____ .

Ruth 1:6

⁶ Then she arose with her daughters-in-law to return from the country of Moab, for she had heard in the fields of Moab that the Lᴏʀᴅ had visited his people and given them food.

```
A story with one promise for
God's people:
```

God takes sorrowful tragedy and turns

it into surprising _____ .

```
We may think that God is _____ from
us...
```

When we are surrounded by famine

or everything seems _____ .

When death strikes or _____ sinks in.

Amidst barrenness and _____ .

In our grief and in our _____ .

But God will show Himself _____ to us.

Ruth 1:22b

And they came to Bethlehem at the beginning
of barley harvest.

His grace will cover our _____.

His mercy will overcome our _____.

"God Moves in a Mysterious Way"
William Cowper, 1774

God moves in a mysterious way,
his wonders to perform;
He plants his footsteps in the sea,
and rides upon the storm.

Deep in unfathomable mines
of never failing skill,
He treasures up his bright designs
and works his sovereign will.

Ye fearful saints, fresh courage take,
the clouds ye so much dread
are big with mercy, and shall break
in blessings on your head.

Judge not the Lord by feeble sense,
but trust him for his grace;
Behind a frowning providence,
he hides a smiling face.

His purpose will ripen fast,
unfolding every hour;
The bud may have bitter taste,
but sweet will be the flower.

Blind unbelief is sure to err,
and scan his work in vain:
God is his own interpreter,
and he will make it plain.

Secret Church

PRAY FOR THE SUFFERING AND TRIALS OF THE PEOPLE WITHOUT THE GOSPEL IN THE RED ZONES (SPIRITUAL AND PHYSICAL NEEDS OF ALL PEOPLE)

- Many people in the red zones in places like India, Indonesia, Afghanistan will be born, live, and die without ever hearing the good news of Jesus Christ. Let's pray that they would hear the truth of God's Word and would trust in Christ.

- Pray for the millions of young people in countries like Turkey, China, and Japan who are wrapped up in secularism and agnosticism.

- Pray for people living in places like Chad that have a great need for clean water and food security.

- Pray for the estimated 27 million victims of human trafficking worldwide at any given time. The majority of countries where this is most prevalent are in red zones. Let's pray for ministries in these areas.

Give Today ♥
Support work in North Korea, Cambodia, Indonesia, and other persecuted places

RADICAL.NET/SCGIVE

RUTH
MEETS BOAZ

Ruth 2:1

¹ Now Naomi had a relative of her husband's, a worthy man of the clan of Elimelech, whose name was Boaz.

Judges 6:12

¹² And the angel of the LORD appeared to him and said to him, "The LORD is with you, O mighty man of valor."

Ruth 2:2

² And Ruth the Moabite said to Naomi, "Let me go to the field and glean among the ears of grain after him in whose sight I shall find favor." And she said to her, "Go, my daughter."

Leviticus 23:22

22 "And when you reap the harvest of your land, you shall not reap your field right up to its edge, nor shall you gather the gleanings after your harvest. You shall leave them for the poor and for the sojourner: I am the LORD your God."

Ruth 2:3

3 So she set out and went and gleaned in the field after the reapers, and she happened to come to the part of the field belonging to Boaz, who was of the clan of Elimelech.

Ruth 2:4

4 And behold, Boaz came from Bethlehem. And he said to the reapers, "The LORD be with you!" And they answered, "The LORD bless you."

Ruth 2:5

5 Then Boaz said to his young man who was in charge of the reapers, "Whose young woman is this?"

Ruth 2:6-7

6 And the servant who was in charge of the reapers answered, "She is the young Moabite woman, who came back with Naomi from the country of Moab. 7 She said, 'Please let me glean and gather among the sheaves after the reapers.' So she came, and she has continued from early morning until now, except for a short rest."

Ruth 2:8

8 Then Boaz said to Ruth, "Now, listen, my daughter, do not go to glean in another field or leave this one, but keep close to my young women.

Ruth 2:9

⁹ Let your eyes be on the field that they are reaping, and go after them. Have I not charged the young men not to touch you? And when you are thirsty, go to the vessels and drink what the young men have drawn."

Ruth 1:14

¹⁴ Then they lifted up their voices and wept again. And Orpah kissed her mother-in-law, but Ruth clung to her.

Ruth 2:10

¹⁰ Then she fell on her face, bowing to the ground, and said to him, "Why have I found favor in your eyes, that you should take notice of me, since I am a foreigner?"

....

....

....

....

....

....

....

....

....

....

....

....

....

....

....

....

....

....

....

....

....

....

....

....

Ruth 2:11-12

[11] But Boaz answered her, "All that you have done for your mother-in-law since the death of your husband has been fully told to me, and how you left your father and mother and your native land and came to a people that you did not know before. [12] The LORD repay you for what you have done, and a full reward be given you by the LORD, the God of Israel, under whose wings you have come to take refuge!"

Ruth 2:13

[13] Then she said, "I have found favor in your eyes, my lord, for you have comforted me and spoken kindly to your servant, though I am not one of your servants."

Ruth 2:14

¹⁴ And at mealtime Boaz said to her, "Come here and eat some bread and dip your morsel in the wine." So she sat beside the reapers, and he passed to her roasted grain. And she ate until she was satisfied, and she had some left over.

Ruth 2:15-16

¹⁵ When she rose to glean, Boaz instructed his young men, saying, "Let her glean even among the sheaves, and do not reproach her. ¹⁶ And also pull out some from the bundles for her and leave it for her to glean, and do not rebuke her."

Ruth 2:17

¹⁷ So she gleaned in the field until evening. Then she beat out what she had gleaned, and it was about an ephah of barley.

....
....
....
....
....
....
....
....
....
....
....
....
....
....
....
....
....
....
....
....
....
....
....
....
....
....

Ruth 2:18

18 And she took it up and went into the city. Her mother-in-law saw what she had gleaned. She also brought out and gave her what food she had left over after being satisfied.

Ruth 2:19

19 And her mother-in-law said to her, "Where did you glean today? And where have you worked? Blessed be the man who took notice of you." So she told her mother-in-law with whom she had worked and said, "The man's name with whom I worked today is Boaz."

Ruth 2:20

²⁰ And Naomi said to her daughter-in-law, "May he be blessed by the Lᴏʀᴅ, whose kindness has not forsaken the living or the dead!" Naomi also said to her, "The man is a close relative of ours, one of our redeemers."

Genesis 48:15-16

¹⁵ And he blessed Joseph and said,

The God before whom my fathers Abraham and Isaac walked,

the God who has been my shepherd all my life long to this day,

¹⁶ the angel who has redeemed me from all evil, bless the boys;

and in them let my name be carried on, and the name of my fathers Abraham and Isaac;

and let them grow into a multitude in the midst of the earth."

....

....

....

....

....

....

....

....

....

....

....

....

....

....

....

....

....

....

....

....

....

....

....

Exodus 6:2-7

2 God spoke to Moses and said to him, "I am the LORD. 3 I appeared to Abraham, to Isaac, and to Jacob, as God Almighty, but by my name the LORD I did not make myself known to them. 4 I also established my covenant with them to give them the land of Canaan, the land in which they lived as sojourners. 5 Moreover, I have heard the groaning of the people of Israel whom the Egyptians hold as slaves, and I have remembered my covenant. 6 Say therefore to the people of Israel, 'I am the LORD, and I will bring you out from under the burdens of the Egyptians, and I will deliver you from slavery to them, and I will redeem you with an outstretched arm and with great acts of judgment. 7 I will take you to be my people, and I will be your God, and you shall know that I am the LORD your God, who has brought you out from under the burdens of the Egyptians.

Leviticus 25:25-27

25 "If your brother becomes poor and sells part of his property, then his nearest redeemer shall come and redeem what his brother has sold. 26 If a man has no one to redeem it and then himself becomes prosperous and finds sufficient means to redeem it, 27 let him calculate the years since he sold it and pay back the balance to the man to whom he sold it, and then return to his property.

Ruth 2:21

21 And Ruth the Moabite said, "Besides, he said to me, 'You shall keep close by my young men until they have finished all my harvest.'"

....
....
....
....
....
....
....
....
....
....
....
....
....
....
....
....
....
....
....
....
....
....
....
....
....
....

Ruth 2:22-23

22 And Naomi said to Ruth, her daughter-in-law, "It is good, my daughter, that you go out with his young women, lest in another field you be assaulted." 23 So she kept close to the young women of Boaz, gleaning until the end of the barley and wheat harvests. And she lived with her mother-in-law.

Ruth 2:20b

"May he be blessed by the LORD, whose kindness has not forsaken the living or the dead."

Hesed

Hesed describes a kind of love, loyalty, kindness, faithfulness and commitment that leads to merciful and compassion action on behalf of another.

RUTH 2 | SESSION 2

_____ in the *hesed* of God in your life.

God _____ you as his _____ .

Deuteronomy 33:26–27a

26   "There is none like God, O Jeshurun,

         who rides through the heavens to your help,

         through the skies in his majesty.

27   The eternal God is your dwelling place,

         and underneath are the everlasting arms.

God _____ you under his _____ .

Psalm 91:1, 4b

1   He who dwells in the shelter of the Most High

     will abide in the shadow of the Almighty.

4   ...Under his wings you will find refuge;

Secret Church   49

God _____ you at his _____.

God _____ you with his _____.

Philippians 4:19

[19] And my God will supply every need of yours according to his riches in glory in Christ Jesus.

In the midst of our _____, the *hesed* of God reminds us that he is _____.

_____ the *hesed* of God through your life.

Seek others in need like family.

Ruth 1:6

⁶ Then she arose with her daughters-in-law to return from the country of Moab, for she had heard in the fields of Moab that the LORD had visited his people and given them food.

James 1:27

²⁷ Religion that is pure and undefiled before God the Father is this: to visit orphans and widows in their affliction, and to keep oneself unstained from the world.

Shelter others in need with love.

Serve others in need at your table.

Shower others in need with grace.

Secret Church

PRAY FOR THE PERSECUTED CHURCH IN THE RED ZONES (MINISTRY CHALLENGES FOR LOCAL BELIEVERS)

- Pray for those who come to faith in areas of the world where conversion to Christianity is illegal, as they often face isolation from their families and communities, political and social constraints, imprisonment, and even death.

- Pray for churches that struggle to meet and carry out the duties of the church because of the constant threat of persecution.

- Pray for believers and seekers in Central Asia and the Middle East who desire to know more about the Bible and desperately need community with other believers who can teach them, yet they fear revealing their identity and don't know who to trust.

- Pray for seminary students in East Asia who cannot study openly in their home context but desire to see the gospel spread and churches planted in their region.

Give Today♥
Support work in North Korea, Cambodia, Indonesia, and other persecuted places

`RADICAL.NET/SCGIVE`

RUTH AND BOAZ
AT THE THRESHING FLOOR

Ruth 3:1

[1] Then Naomi her mother-in-law said to her, "My daughter, should I not seek rest for you, that it may be well with you?

Ruth 3:2

[2] Is not Boaz our relative, with whose young women you were? See, he is winnowing barley tonight at the threshing floor.

Ruth 3:3-4

[3] Wash therefore and anoint yourself, and put on your cloak and go down to the threshing floor, but do not make yourself known to the man until he has finished eating and drinking. [4] But when he lies down, observe the place where he lies. Then go and uncover his feet and lie down, and he will tell you what to do."

2 Samuel 12:20a

[20] Then David arose from the earth and washed and anointed himself and changed his clothes. And he went into the house of the LORD and worshiped.

Ruth 3:5

[5] And she replied, "All that you say I will do."

Ruth 3:6-7a

[6] So she went down to the threshing floor and did just as her mother-in-law had commanded her. [7] And when Boaz had eaten and drunk, and his heart was merry, he went to lie down at the end of the heap of grain.

Ruth 3:7b

Then she came softly and uncovered his feet and lay down.

Ruth 3:8

[8] At midnight the man was startled and turned over, and behold, a woman lay at his feet!

Ruth 3:9a

[9] He said, "Who are you?" And she answered, "I am Ruth, your servant.

Ruth 2:13

[13] Then she said, "I have found favor in your eyes, my lord, for you have comforted me and spoken kindly to your servant, though I am not one of your servants."

Ruth 3:9b

Spread your wings over your servant, for you are a redeemer."

Ruth 2:12

12 The LORD repay you for what you have done, and a full reward be given you by the LORD, the God of Israel, under whose wings you have come to take refuge!"

Ruth 3:10

10 And he said, "May you be blessed by the LORD, my daughter. You have made this last kindness greater than the first in that you have not gone after young men, whether poor or rich.

Ruth 3:11

11 And now, my daughter, do not fear. I will do for you all that you ask, for all my fellow townsmen know that you are a worthy woman.

....

....

....

....

....

....

....

....

....

....

....

....

....

....

....

....

....

....

....

....

....

....

....

Proverbs 31:10

10   An excellent wife who can find?

      She is far more precious than jewels.

Proverbs 31:31

31   Give her of the fruit of her hands,

      and let her works praise her in the gates.

Ruth 3:12

12 And now it is true that I am a redeemer.

Yet there is a redeemer nearer than I.

Ruth 3:13

13 Remain tonight, and in the morning, if he will

redeem you, good; let him do it. But if he is not

willing to redeem you, then, as the LORD lives,

I will redeem you. Lie down until the morning."

Ruth 3:14

[14] So she lay at his feet until the morning, but arose before one could recognize another. And he said, "Let it not be known that the woman came to the threshing floor."

Ruth 3:15 °

[15] And he said, "Bring the garment you are wearing and hold it out." So she held it, and he measured out six measures of barley and put it on her. Then she went into the city.

Ruth 3:16

[16] And when she came to her mother-in-law, she said, "How did you fare, my daughter?" Then she told her all that the man had done for her,

Ruth 3:17

[17] saying, "These six measures of barley he gave to me, for he said to me, 'You must not go back empty-handed to your mother-in-law.'"

Ruth 1:21a

[21] I went away full, and the Lord has brought me back empty.

Ruth 3:18

[18] She replied, "Wait, my daughter, until you learn how the matter turns out, for the man will not rest but will settle the matter today."

Ruth 3:10

[10] And he said, "May you be blessed by the LORD, my daughter. You have made this last kindness greater than the first in that you have not gone after young men, whether poor or rich.

5 Biblical Characteristics of Love

Love is _____ .

1 Corinthians 13:4-8a

[4] Love is patient and kind; love does not envy or boast; it is not arrogant [5] or rude. It does not insist on its own way; it is not irritable or resentful; [6] it does not rejoice at wrongdoing, but rejoices with the truth. [7] Love bears all things, believes all things, hopes all things, endures all things. [8] Love never ends.

Love is _____.

Genesis 19:30-32

[30] Now Lot went up out of Zoar and lived in the hills with his two daughters, for he was afraid to live in Zoar. So he lived in a cave with his two daughters. [31] And the firstborn said to the younger, "Our father is old, and there is not a man on earth to come in to us after the manner of all the earth. [32] Come, let us make our father drink wine, and we will lie with him, that we may preserve offspring from our father."

Genesis 19:33

[33] So they made their father drink wine that night. And the firstborn went in and lay with her father. He did not know when she lay down or when she arose.

Genesis 19:34-36

34 The next day, the firstborn said to the younger, "Behold, I lay last night with my father. Let us make him drink wine tonight also. Then you go in and lie with him, that we may preserve offspring from our father." 35 So they made their father drink wine that night also. And the younger arose and lay with him, and he did not know when she lay down or when she arose. 36 Thus both the daughters of Lot became pregnant by their father.

Genesis 19:37

37 The firstborn bore a son and called his name Moab. He is the father of the Moabites to this day.

Love _____ .

Love _____ .

Love pays a _____ .

Challenge: Identify 1-3 ways you can grow in your love for others.

PRAY FOR MINISTRY EFFORTS IN THE RED ZONES (EVANGELISM, PASTOR TRAINING, AND CHURCH PLANTING).

- Pray for the leaders of college campus ministries in East Asia who are spreading the gospel and helping new believers grow in their faith. Pray for Southeast Asian church planters as they are being equipped and prepared to carry out the ministry that God has called them to.

- Pray for ministry workers who are creating and posting culturally relevant, thought-provoking content on social media platforms to engage seekers with the gospel and connect believers with follow-up groups.

- Pray that more pastors in the red zones would have access to solid, biblical teaching, resources, and programs that train them to preach faithfully from God's Word.

- Pray that we would see more Asian believers being trained to move across cultures as missionaries. Pray that these trainees will be equipped to take the gospel to people and places in restrictive-access countries where Christ is little-known.

- Pray that we would be able to provide a theologically sound training for local church leaders and encourage church leaders and pastors to more faithfully engage their local communities with the gospel.

- Pray for small business projects to provide steady income and ministry opportunities for local believers and to ultimately provide gospel access to unreached people groups in Southeast Asia.

Give Today ♥
Support work in North Korea, Cambodia, Indonesia, and other persecuted places

`RADICAL.NET/SCGIVE`

BOAZ
REDEEMS RUTH

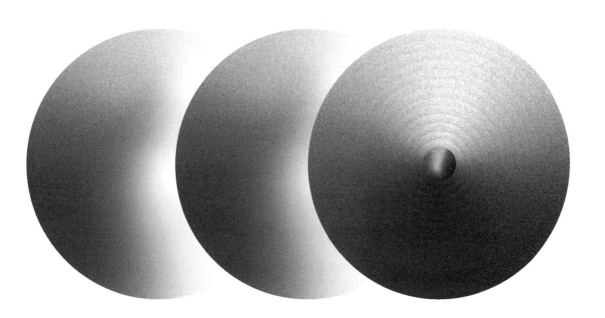

Ruth 4:1a

[1] Now Boaz had gone up to the gate and sat down there. And behold, the redeemer, of whom Boaz had spoken, came by.

Deuteronomy 25:5-10

[5] "If brothers dwell together, and one of them dies and has no son, the wife of the dead man shall not be married outside the family to a stranger. Her husband's brother shall go in to her and take her as his wife and perform the duty of a husband's brother to her. [6] And the first son whom she bears shall succeed to the name of his dead brother, that his name may not be blotted out of Israel. [7] And if the man does not wish to take his brother's wife, then his brother's wife shall go up to the gate to the elders and say, 'My husband's brother refuses to perpetuate his brother's name in Israel; he will not perform the duty of a husband's brother to me.'

⁸ Then the elders of his city shall call him and speak to him, and if he persists, saying, 'I do not wish to take her,' ⁹ then his brother's wife shall go up to him in the presence of the elders and pull his sandal off his foot and spit in his face. And she shall answer and say, 'So shall it be done to the man who does not build up his brother's house.' ¹⁰ And the name of his house shall be called in Israel, 'The house of him who had his sandal pulled off.'

Ruth 4:1b

So Boaz said, "Turn aside, friend; sit down here." And he turned aside and sat down.

Ruth 4:2

² And he took ten men of the elders of the city and said, "Sit down here." So they sat down.

Ruth 4:3-4

³ Then he said to the redeemer, "Naomi, who has come back from the country of Moab, is selling the parcel of land that belonged to our relative Elimelech. ⁴ So I thought I would tell you of it and say, 'Buy it in the presence of those sitting here and in the presence of the elders of my people.' If you will redeem it, redeem it. But if you will not, tell me, that I may know, for there is no one besides you to redeem it, and I come after you." And he said, "I will redeem it."

Ruth 4:5

⁵ Then Boaz said, "The day you buy the field from the hand of Naomi, you also acquire Ruth the Moabite, the widow of the dead, in order to perpetuate the name of the dead in his inheritance."

Ruth 4:6

6 Then the redeemer said, "I cannot redeem it for myself, lest I impair my own inheritance. Take my right of redemption yourself, for I cannot redeem it."

Ruth 4:7-8

7 Now this was the custom in former times in Israel concerning redeeming and exchanging: to confirm a transaction, the one drew off his sandal and gave it to the other, and this was the manner of attesting in Israel. 8 So when the redeemer said to Boaz, "Buy it for yourself," he drew off his sandal.

....

....

....

....

....

....

....

....

....

....

....

....

....

....

....

....

....

....

....

....

....

....

Ruth 4:9

9 Then Boaz said to the elders and all the people, "You are witnesses this day that I have bought from the hand of Naomi all that belonged to Elimelech and all that belonged to Chilion and to Mahlon.

Ruth 4:10

10 Also Ruth the Moabite, the widow of Mahlon, I have bought to be my wife, to perpetuate the name of the dead in his inheritance, that the name of the dead may not be cut off from among his brothers and from the gate of his native place. You are witnesses this day."

Ruth 4:11-12

11 Then all the people who were at the gate and the elders said, "We are witnesses. May the LORD make the woman, who is coming into your

house, like Rachel and Leah, who together built up the house of Israel. May you act worthily in Ephrathah and be renowned in Bethlehem, [12] and may your house be like the house of Perez, whom Tamar bore to Judah, because of the offspring that the LORD will give you by this young woman."

Ruth 4:13

[13] So Boaz took Ruth, and she became his wife. And he went in to her, and the LORD gave her conception, and she bore a son.

Ruth 1:6

[6] Then she arose with her daughters-in-law to return from the country of Moab, for she had heard in the fields of Moab that the LORD had visited his people and given them food.

The LORD is the only One who can

_____ for our deepest needs.

Ruth 4:14

[14] Then the women said to Naomi, "Blessed be the LORD, who has not left you this day without a redeemer, and may his name be renowned in Israel!

Ruth 4:15

[15] He shall be to you a restorer of life and a nourisher of your old age, for your daughter-in-law who loves you, who is more to you than seven sons, has given birth to him."

Ruth 4:16

[16] Then Naomi took the child and laid him on her lap and became his nurse.

Ruth 4:17

¹⁷ And the women of the neighborhood gave him a name, saying, "A son has been born to Naomi." They named him Obed. He was the father of Jesse, the father of David.

Ruth 4:18-22

¹⁸ Now these are the generations of Perez: Perez fathered Hezron, ¹⁹ Hezron fathered Ram, Ram fathered Amminadab, ²⁰ Amminadab fathered Nahshon, Nahshon fathered Salmon, ²¹ Salmon fathered Boaz, Boaz fathered Obed, ²² Obed fathered Jesse, and Jesse fathered David.

....
....
....
....
....
....
....
....
....
....
....
....
....
....
....
....
....
....
....
....
....
....
....
....

Requirements of a Redeemer

The_____ to redeem.

The_____ to redeem.

The_____ to redeem.

Pictures of Redemption

God brings his people from death to _____.

God brings his people from curse to _____.

God brings his people from bitterness
to _____.

God brings his people from emptiness
to _____.

God brings his people from despair to _____.

Matthew 1:5-6a

⁵ and Salmon the father of Boaz by Rahab, and Boaz the father of Obed by Ruth, and Obed the father of Jesse, ⁶ and Jesse the father of David the king.

Matthew 1:16

¹⁶ and Jacob the father of Joseph the husband of Mary, of whom Jesus was born, who is called Christ.

Our Hope of Redemption

The story of Ruth is not ultimately about redemption for Naomi and Ruth through a baby born in Bethlehem named _____.

The story of Ruth is ultimately about redemption for you and me through another baby born in Bethlehem named _____.

A Redeemer Has Come

Jesus has the _____ to redeem us.

John 1:14

[14] And the Word became flesh and dwelt among us, and we have seen his glory, glory as of the only Son from the Father, full of grace and truth.

Philippians 2:5-7

[5] Have this mind among yourselves, which is yours in Christ Jesus, [6] who, though he was in the form of God, did not count equality with God a thing to be grasped, [7] but emptied himself, by taking the form of a servant, being born in the likeness of men.

Hebrews 4:15

[15] For we do not have a high priest who is unable to sympathize with our weaknesses, but one who in every respect has been tempted as we are, yet without sin.

Jesus has the_____to redeem us.

Colossians 1:15-17

¹⁵ He is the image of the invisible God, the firstborn of all creation. ¹⁶ For by him all things were created, in heaven and on earth, visible and invisible, whether thrones or dominions or rulers or authorities—all things were created through him and for him. ¹⁷ And he is before all things, and in him all things hold together.

Hebrews 1:3

³ He is the radiance of the glory of God and the exact imprint of his nature, and he upholds the universe by the word of his power.

Jesus has the _____ to redeem us.

Galatians 3:13

[13] Christ redeemed us from the curse of the law by becoming a curse for us—for it is written, "Cursed is everyone who is hanged on a tree"—

Galatians 4:4b-5

God sent forth his Son, born of woman, born under the law, [5] to redeem those who were under the law, so that we might receive adoption as sons.

Ephesians 1:7

[7] In him we have redemption through his blood, the forgiveness of our trespasses, according to the riches of his grace,

Titus 2:13-14

[13] waiting for our blessed hope, the appearing of the glory of our great God and Savior Jesus Christ, [14] who gave himself for us to redeem us from all lawlessness and to purify for himself a people for his own possession who are zealous for good works.

Colossians 1:13-14

[13] He has delivered us from the domain of darkness and transferred us to the kingdom of his beloved Son, [14] in whom we have redemption, the forgiveness of sins.

For all who trust in Jesus as Redeemer...

We always have hope because our Redeemer will always _____ for his people.

....
....
....
....
....
....
....
....
....
....
....
....
....
....
....
....
....
....
....
....
....
....
....

Isaiah 43:1-3a

1 But now thus says the LORD,

he who created you, O Jacob,

he who formed you, O Israel:

"Fear not, for I have redeemed you;

I have called you by name, you are mine.

2 When you pass through the waters, I will be

with you; and through the rivers, they shall

not overwhelm you;

when you walk through fire you shall not be

burned, and the flame shall not consume you.

3 For I am the LORD your God,

the Holy One of Israel, your Savior.

"Why is it that we want every chapter to be good when God promises only that in the last chapter he will make all the other chapters make sense, and he doesn't promise we'll see that last chapter here?"

— Steve Saint

Job 19:25-26

25 For I know that my Redeemer lives, and at the last he will stand upon the earth. 26 And after my skin has been thus destroyed, yet in my flesh I shall see God,

We live and die to spread _____ because our Redeemer is radically pursuing all peoples.

Revelation 5:1-2

1 Then I saw in the right hand of him who was seated on the throne a scroll written within and on the back, sealed with seven seals. 2 And I saw a mighty angel proclaiming with a loud voice, "Who is worthy to open the scroll and break its seals?"

Revelation 5:3-4

3 And no one in heaven or on earth or under the earth was able to open the scroll or to look into it, 4 and I began to weep loudly because no one was found worthy to open the scroll or to look into it.

....
....
....
....
....
....
....
....
....
....
....
....
....
....
....
....
....
....
....
....
....
....
....
....

Revelation 5:5

5 And one of the elders said to me, "Weep no more; behold, the Lion of the tribe of Judah, the Root of David, has conquered, so that he can open the scroll and its seven seals."

Revelation 5:6-13

6 And between the throne and the four living creatures and among the elders I saw a Lamb standing, as though it had been slain, with seven horns and with seven eyes, which are the seven spirits of God sent out into all the earth. 7 And he went and took the scroll from the right hand of him who was seated on the throne.

8 And when he had taken the scroll, the four living creatures and the twenty-four elders fell down before the Lamb, each holding a harp, and golden bowls full of incense, which are the prayers of the saints.

⁹ And they sang a new song, saying,

"Worthy are you to take the scroll

and to open its seals,

for you were slain, and by your blood you

ransomed people for God

from every tribe and language and people

and nation,

¹⁰ and you have made them a kingdom and

priests to our God,

and they shall reign on the earth."

¹¹ Then I looked, and I heard around the throne
and the living creatures and the elders the voice
of many angels, numbering myriads of myriads and
thousands of thousands, ¹² saying with a loud voice,

"Worthy is the Lamb who was slain,

to receive power and wealth and wisdom and

might and honor and glory and blessing!"

¹³ And I heard every creature in heaven and on earth
and under the earth and in the sea, and all that is in
them, saying,

"To him who sits on the throne and to the

Lamb be blessing and honor and glory and

might forever and ever!"

From Ruth to Matthew to Revelation, Jesus our Redeemer is radically pursuing all tribes, languages, peoples, and nations.

"There Is a Fountain"
William Cowper, 1772

There is a fountain filled with blood,
Drawn from Immanuel's veins,
And sinners plunged beneath that flood
Lose all their guilty stains.

The dying thief rejoiced to see
That fountain in his day;
And there have I, though vile as he,
Washed all my sins away.

Dear dying Lamb, Thy precious blood
Shall never lose its pow'r,
Till all the ransomed church of God
Are safe, to sin no more.

E'er since by faith I saw the stream
Thy flowing wounds supply,
Redeeming love has been my theme,
And shall be till I die.

When this poor, lisping, stamm'ring tongue
Lies silent in the grave,
Then in a nobler, sweeter song,
I'll sing Thy pow'r to save.

PRAYER MOMENT

....

....

....

....

....

....

....

....

....

....

....

....

....

....

....

....

....

....

....

....

Give Today
Support work in North Korea, Cambodia,
Indonesia, and other persecuted places

RADICAL.NET/SCGIVE

ANSWER KEY

SESSION 1

p. 29 - promise, compromise, hurt, devotion

p. 30 - food, family, great, good

p. 31 - triumph, far, foreign, despair, loneliness, shame

p. 32 - faithful, sin, sorrow

SESSION 2

p. 49 - Rest, seeks, family, shelters, wings

p. 50 - serves, table, showers, grace, waiting, working, Reflect

SESSION 3

p. 63 - patient

p. 64 - pure

p. 65 - protects, provides, price

SESSION 4

p. 76 - provide

p. 78 - right, resources, resolve, life, blessing, happiness, fullness, hope

p. 79 - Obed, Jesus

p. 80 - right

p. 81 - resources

p. 82 - resolve

p. 83 - provide

p. 85 - hope

NOTES

2006 2007 2008 2009 2010 2011 2012 2013 2014 2015 2016 2017 2018 2019 2020 2021 2022 **2023 →**

EXPLORE 23 PAST SECRET CHURCH EVENTS

CONTENT AVAILABLE FOR FREE!

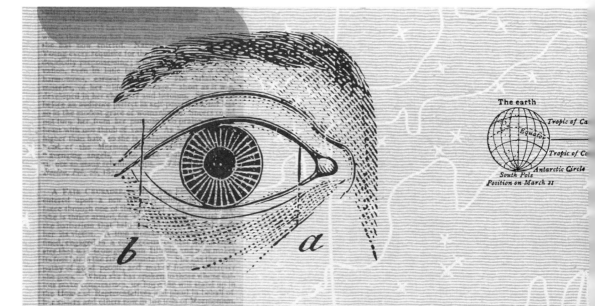

The earth
Tropic of Ca
Equator
Tropic of C
Antarctic Circle
South Pole
Position on March 21

In Plain Sight

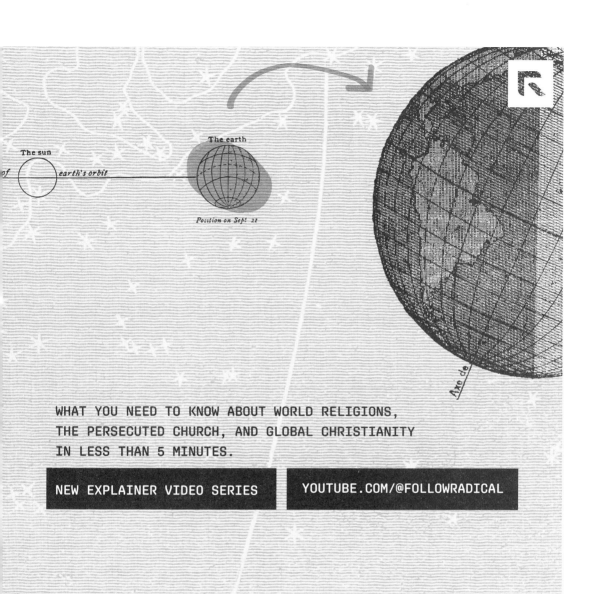

WHAT YOU NEED TO KNOW ABOUT WORLD RELIGIONS,
THE PERSECUTED CHURCH, AND GLOBAL CHRISTIANITY
IN LESS THAN 5 MINUTES.

NEW EXPLAINER VIDEO SERIES   YOUTUBE.COM/@FOLLOWRADICAL